An Educator's Journey to a Successful School

Moving a Failing School to Success

by

Leary B. Adams Jr., Ed.D.

DORRANCE
PUBLISHING CO
EST. 1920
PITTSBURGH, PENNSYLVANIA 15238

Dorrance Publishing Co
585 Alpha Drive
Pittsburgh, PA 15238
Visit our website at www.dorrancebookstore.com

ISBN: 978-1-6366-1227-0
EISBN: 978-1-6366-1814-2

This book is dedicated to:

My beautiful and supportive wife, Regina. "The glue that holds our family together."

Also, the men and women, professional educators, professional support staff, and the community that was a part of our school's journey to excellence. A no-excuse school prepared to meet the needs of any child crossing our threshold. We were in fact a family working towards a common goal…the education of "Every Child."

Contents

Introduction

An Educator's Journey to a Successful School: Moving a Failing School to Success was written to shed light on the adage that education is both an art and science. Albert Einstein explained it best when saying, "everything that can be counted doesn't count and everything that counts can't be counted." The art being the passion, love, and heart that a dedicated professional educator puts into their craft to make a difference with every child. The science being the research-based best practices used to ensure lessons are delivered to every student in the most effective way. The professional educator, putting both the art and science together to support every child in becoming their best self is one of those true miracles that can be witnessed in our lifetime.

This book will take you on a journey. A journey incorporating strategies of both art and science to reach the goal of a highly effective school community. You will learn strategies that can be used to build a culture of professional educators in your school and strategies to raise academic achievement of all students.

My journey began as a new principal assigned to the lowest achieving school in my state. I quickly realized that if I were going to make a difference, I would have to learn the art and science of turning around a desperately failing school. While doing the absolute best I could for my school community, I also began to work towards my Doctor of Education Degree. The building management aspect of the job was not too difficult in that I had previously been a successful and decorated military officer. Receiving commendations for outstanding duty, being assigned to a marginal duty station, and moving it to exceptional within one Inspector General cycle, I felt like I had been in this situation before. However, the responsibility for the management of personnel and security of structures and assets did not prepare me for the ultimate job of raising student achievement.

As I moved through my Doctor of Education Degree, I was able to research and learn strategies and tactics of a different type of battle. The battle against failure. The battle against failing schools, adults failing children, failing dreams, and failing futures. Schools serving as a pipeline to the criminal justice system.

I had a new mission… and my mission was to be as successful within my school as I was in my military career. I approached it as if it were a life-and-death situation, and for many of our children, without a good education, it could literally mean life or death.

It is my hope that as you follow me on this journey towards school improvement you will find some art and science of education that you can use for the benefit of students in your school.

Building a Culture
of Professional Educators

*"Treat people as if they were what they ought to be, and you
may help them to become what they are capable of being."*
Johann Wolfgang von Goethe

I find myself using the term professional educator more and more. The term teacher just does not do justice to the many hours of dedication and skill required to be an effective educator. **Professional educators work endlessly before and after contract hours because like artists, professional educators strive from the heart to produce their absolute best work.** That work is an educated child ready to move to the next level of the educational process or with the confidence and skills necessary to meet the demands of the workplace and society in general. We hold in our hands and in our control the future of our nation and the future of individuals. We know all too well the negative effects associated with a poor education or non-completion, i.e. dropping out.

Building a culture of professional educators must begin with mutual respect. Mutual respect between teachers, students, administrators, parents, and other stakeholders is essential to build the foundation for a culture of professionalism. It is critical to the success of our students that we find ways to get past the "them versus us" syndrome that is sometimes encountered between the most important stakeholders in our schools. The educational leader must set the example for communicating and listening to all stakeholders and constantly work on developing those skills necessary to ensure everyone understands their importance in the education of our children. When we can put everything else aside and base our decisions on what is best for student achievement, then and only then, will we become a team of professional educators working in a professional setting.

It is incumbent upon the school administrator to take the lead in **molding the culture of professionalism.** The administrator must collaborate with other professional educators on issues relevant to student achievement. This should include educators not only inside, but also educators outside of your immediate building. This is not a one-man or woman show. This collaboration or "collective leadership" can come in the form of school improvement teams, vertical articulation groups, response to intervention teams, structured teacher planning time, grade level meetings or whatever the DNA of your school requires. Remember, this is about collaborating on issues relevant to student achievement. Whatever name you choose to give your team is not as important as the results gained by the minds of multiple professional educators coming together to form a cohesive strategic plan for student achievement. Not only are you engaging in shared leadership, but you are also **developing your future instructional leaders** as they assist in the development of the blueprint for your strategic plan.

Take every opportunity to **provide additional compensation** to professional educators going above and beyond the call of duty and achieving exceptional results. Getting exceptional results requires numerous hours spent preparing effective lessons and assessments; monitoring student progress; planning interventions for those needing additional assistance; and continuing to do the things necessary to perfect the art and science of teaching. Let us not forget, we are tasked with educating those that will be required to lead the greatest country on earth.

Praise and celebrate the progress made in student achievement. Praise educators for working together as professionals. Thank them for dedicating themselves to a job that has so many variables that are out of their control. Praise educators for being professional enough to accept the challenges of educating all children and continue to successfully do one of, if not the toughest jobs in the world. Celebrate and praise educators for all accomplishments and progress made; end of chapter test results; interim assessments; formative and summative assessments; positive classroom observations; and even positive conversations you may have overheard. Remember…**praise in public but do your redirection individually as necessary.**

Above all, make sure you **model the leadership traits you expect of others.** The educational leader must always be fair and ethical and will accept nothing less from those in the organization. The ethical responsibilities of educational leaders in schools are to follow the policies and regulations of the organization, question those policies and regulations if they do not conform to basic values, and to provide each student and staff member with an equal opportunity to learn and develop.

The choices we face while doing our jobs could be a lot easier if we were shallow persons with no basic values. However, as noted by Rushworth Kidder (1996) in *How Good People make Tough Choices*, "sound values raise tough choices; and tough choices are never easy." It has become obvious to me that the toughest choices involve situations of right versus right. We choose different paths based on deep-rooted basic core values. In many cases situations can be argued from different sides with each side passionately believing their own solution to be correct. Correct becomes a matter of personal ethics based on individual core values.

As an administrator, teacher, and educational leader, I have concluded that some decisions based on right versus right must also be decided by weighing the core values of the community and the political climate of your environment at the time of the decision. Are the core values of the community or the political climate able to tolerate the decision being made? This must be considered as an ethical responsibility for the educational leader.

You must be on your "A" game even when you feel that it may be less than an "A" day. Remember, **you set the climate and that climate must be positive, fair, ethical, hopeful, and upbeat always.**

Takeaway from Building Culture
- **Building a positive culture must begin with mutual respect for ALL stakeholders.**
- **Administrators must take the lead when it comes to modeling the culture of professionalism.**

In the next section we will discuss the importance of developing a vision and living that vision.

Vision

"Anyone can steer the ship, but it takes a real leader to chart the course."

George Barna

E leanor Roosevelt put vision into perspective when she said, **"The future belongs to those who believe in the beauty of their dreams."** The vision of an organization is the dream of that organization. **"What does your school stand for?"** and "Where is the school going?" are questions that cannot be answered without having a vision. What dream could inspire the entire educational community to work for the betterment of the whole, and rally them to commit to the same goals and values? That dream is the vision.

A shared vision by all members of the school will allow them to set goals for the improvement of all students. Lucas (1998) sees **shared vision as a force that "compels people to do something, change something, or become something.** It has even been suggested (Godish 2001) that an effective way to communicate the group vision is through a strategic principle that equates to a catchy phrase that defines and guides the organization. Some examples of this strategic principle used by my local school district, "Ready by Exit," the goal being, all students being ready for the next grade or the next stage of life after graduation. "Keep your eye on the CAP." The focus is on Climate, Achievement, and Participation (CAP), with the outcome being the graduation cap. "We are an A+ School District. We stand for Access, Accountability, and Achievement." Some others would be Burger King, "We do it all

5

for you," and Walmart's "Low prices, every day." These strategic principles are not only what these organizations stand for, but also guide the organization towards what is to be accomplished.

Communicating the vision takes more than posting the statement in a frame and placing it on the wall. Your vision will have to be tied to the core values of the group and a living document that is practiced and believed by all the members of the school.

When looking at our schools we must ask ourselves if we are really living up to the vision and core values that we put down on paper? Does our vision statement really reflect what the school in trying to accomplish, and are all the members of the school community aware of and supportive of that vision? Every opportunity must be taken to communicate the vision to staff, parents, students, and the community whenever possible. This can be accomplished through newsletters, stationery, and ending every meeting with the vision statement.

As the educational leaders of our schools **we not only talk of vision, we set the example in everything that we do.** As leaders, if we are not able to create a sense of shared vision and communicate that vision through words and actions, we will never be able to lead our organization in an effective manner.

Takeaway from Vision
- **A shared vision should compel people to do something, change something, or become something.**
- **Educational leaders should not only talk of vision but set the example for that vision in everything they do.**

In the next section we will discuss the importance of knowing your challenges and planning for success.

Planning for Success

"Give me six hours to chop down a tree and I will spend the first four sharpening the ax."

Abraham Lincoln

It has been said that writing a lesson plan is like planning a family vacation. You must decide where you want to go; how you plan on getting there; what you will need for the trip; and how will you know when you have arrived. You would not place your family in harm's way by not planning properly or not attending to every detail to ensure a safe and orderly arrival to your destination. You would expect only the best results for your family. Strategic planning and building a schoolwide learning structure for student achievement should take on many of the same attributes as planning for that family vacation or writing that lesson plan. I have heard a couple of interesting phrases regarding planning, such as the five Ps, proper preparation prevents poor performance, and failing to plan equates to planning to fail. Both are so true when expecting to make a difference in student achievement in the classroom and the school.

Regardless of the most exacting plans, those plans will be worthless if the entire learning community did not have the highest expectations for the achievement of every child. It is the responsibility of the educational leader to ensure every adult and child understands that anything less than excellence will not be accepted. This is not something that can be faked, nor is it something that can be overlooked. Adults and children alike will see through you if you are not sincere about this belief. It will be through communicating, that is, speaking with and listening to the professional educators around you. **The educational leader must consistently reinforce the passion for student achievement** and to identify those that may not have the same expectations for the academic, social, and emotional growth of every child.

Planning can be even more challenging when you are faced with changes in demographics that are swift and unexpected. Schools, like many areas of our society, can change swiftly as if overnight.

Surely, we can all agree, **our classrooms reflect our society.** The changing demographics of our nation and communities reflect what we are seeing in our classrooms. The demographic changes are signals to our educational leaders, professional educators, policy makers, and anyone involved with the education of our children, that we must **adjust our thinking to include and to meet the needs of a more diverse student population.**

Demographics have changed in different ways in different states. My experience is with the changing demographics to a more diverse student population.

It has been said that **to maintain a strong democracy it is important that we maintain an educated populace.** Planning on how we meet the educational challenges ahead of us and how we address our increasingly diverse population will have a significant impact on our nation. At the rate we are going, soon there will be no individual race that will make up over 50 percent, or most of the US population.

While our nation's population is growing more diverse, we are also growing older as a nation. According to the Center for Public Education, non-Hispanic whites are the oldest group of the population; Hispanics are the youngest. Our youngest population is the most diverse, with 47 percent of children younger than five years of age belonging to a racial or ethnic minority group.

These statistics have many implications for our schools and our nation. This data corroborates that nationally, our **school population will be made up of a larger group of children of color and Hispanic origin.** Our workforce to include police, firefighters, teachers, doctors, and all the other professions we depend on for our safety and well-being will increasingly be to a large extent in the hands of those children of color or Hispanic origin.

It is incumbent upon us as educators and as a nation to ensure these students are prepared socially, emotionally, and academically to lead and represent us as we grow older individually and as a nation at large. **The consequences** of us failing to ensure the education of our entire population could lead to serious shortages in many of the professions required to keep us healthy, safe, and strong as a sovereign nation.

In 2000, I was assigned to a school going through a demographic transition. I remained at that school until my retirement in 2014. In the year 2000, the fastest growing states were in the western region of the US. Nevada, where my school was located, was growing faster than all states, by 35.1 percent between 2000 and 2010. According to the US Census Bureau, between these years Nevada's non-Hispanic white population growth change was 12.2 percent; Blacks 61.4 percent; Hispanics 81.9 percent and Asian 116.5 percent.

In a matter of a few years, I saw the demographics of my school change from most non-Hispanic whites to a majority of Black and Hispanic students.

The swift change in demographics and socioeconomic conditions put my school staff in an uncomfortable position. They were uncomfortable because they were not prepared to address the varied needs of our children. Many students were coming from a lower socioeconomic background, in addition to many children having no grasp of academic English or spoke no English at all. **Most of my teachers were non-Hispanic whites and experienced a significant shift in their cultural comfort level and level of expertise for teaching a diverse population of students.**

It became evident that much planning and training of teachers would be necessary to meet the needs of all students.

Takeaway Planning for Success
- **Our classrooms reflect our society.**
- **A strong democracy requires an educated populace.**
- **Our school population will be made up of a larger group of children of color.**

In the next section we will discuss having frank discussions and approaching challenges head-on.

Facing Challenges Head-On

"When we least expect it, life sets us a challenge to test our courage and willingness to change; at such a moment, there is no point in pretending that nothing has happened or in saying that we are not yet ready. The challenge will not wait. Life does not look back."

Paulo Coelho

As my school's demographics changed to predominately children of color, I found it important to have frank discussions regarding the real and perceived challenges of being successful with every student. This was not easy because many teachers were uncomfortable to share their true feelings about educating children from different cultures. **There had to be frank discussions regarding both conscious and unconscious stereotypes that we all carry in our hearts and minds.** If we were going to make a difference, our discussions had to focus on what we felt students would be able to achieve.

Professional educators must feel safe to have candid conversations regarding their feelings and their expectations for all children. The educational leader must be prepared to **address any stereotypes with research and facts relevant to the conversations.** This research should be something done as a learning community with the goal of supporting the fact that **all students are capable of being successful, regardless of the challenges they face, socioeconomic conditions, or the color of their skin.**

Leary B. Adams, Jr., Ed.D

Along with research, a program that I used to bring attention to un-conscious stereotypes is a program that has been around for many years. The Teacher Expectations & Student Achievement Program or TESA provided additional strategies on how to interact with students on a more equitable basis. This approach is based on expectation theory, which says that teachers make inferences about a student's behavior or ability based on what a teacher knows about a student. Sometimes these inferences may be stereotypical and cause the student to match the expectation, and that could be either positive or negative. Tauber in *Self-Fulfilling Prophecy* (1997) states *"Whether it is a student's social class, race, ethnicity, or some combination of these factors that triggers teachers' expectations, the potential for real damage exists. It is important that teachers are aware of the pre-conceived stereotypes that they may bring into their classrooms."* These preconceived stereotypes could become expectations or a *"self-fulfilling prophecy"* (SFP). This term was coined by sociologist Robert K. Merton in 1948 meaning, what you expect is what you will get. Additionally, Ro-senthal and Jacobson (1968) introduced the Pygmalion effect in the class-room, which suggests that **the expectation we have about a person can eventually lead that person to behave in ways that confirm those ex-pectations.**

Both academic and behavioral expectations must be established in the learning community. Those expectations will be developed by the learning community based on established district, state, or national standards, and re-search based. The academic and behavioral expectations must be consistently presented in both verbal and written form to students, parents and all profes-sional and support personnel. Everyone in the learning community will be ac-countable for the expectations established by the learning community. It has been my experience that given an opportunity to collaboratively develop the learning and behavioral expectations most professional educators will not only meet, but in fact exceed those expectations.

Takeaway from Facing Challenges Head-On
- **Frank discussions on conscious and unconscious stereotypes are important.**
- **Stereotypes must be addressed with research and facts.**

12

- **High expectations for all students must be established as the norm.**

In the next section we will discuss the importance of teacher training to meet the needs of all students.

Professional Development

"Growth is the great separator between those who succeed and those who do not. When I see a person beginning to separate themselves from the pack, it's almost always due to personal growth."

John C. Maxwell

When doing professional development, it is important to **start with training associated with the academic and behavioral expectations developed by the learning community.** This training should have the intent of moving teachers to the next level of proficiency as professional educators ready to meet the needs of our clientele, our children. I am sure you are familiar with the adage "teach what we preach." If our strategic plan calls for specific expectations or actions, then that will be our goal for training. Remember to stay focused, and keep your compass pointed in the right direction. The different landscape and the rough seas associated with our profession can make it easy to drift off course.

Becky DuFour stressed that *"the most promising strategy for sustained, substantive school improvement is building the capacity of school personnel to function as a professional learning community. The path to change in the classroom lies within and through professional learning communities."*

We realized that our teachers were not prepared to teach all children. It would be great if every teacher could walk into a classroom with the skills and training necessary to teach every student. That proficiency is not the reality seen by most educational leaders.

15

Try to imagine yourself being a teacher. Can you imagine a student walking into your classroom not being able to speak English? However, your job is to teach the curriculum and the English language? What about the child that is two or three grades below grade level? I could go on and on. **If the educational leader fails to provide teachers with the training necessary to meet the needs of every student, failure for both the teacher and student will be assured.**

There can be many types of professional development going on in a school. There could be new teacher training; second language training; curriculum training; behavioral management training; and far too many to mention here.

As the educational leader it is also important to **differentiate your professional development to reflect the varying levels of experience and needs in the school.** Experienced teachers can play supportive roles in the development of that training. (Remember, this will help them become your next educational leaders.) If training is something to bring new educators up to speed, make sure it is understood that it is geared to new educators. The experienced educators previously trained on the subject can be invited to attend as a refresher. If it is something new that you are introducing to the entire school, then say that it is mandatory for all educators.

Takeaway Professional Development
- **Training should be focused on academic and behavioral expectations developed by the learning community.**
- **Failure to provide necessary training can cause the failure of both teacher and student.**
- **Differentiate training to reflect varying levels of teacher need and experience.**

In the next section we will discuss the importance of not only assessment but also progress-monitoring and providing needed assistance.

Assessment and Progress-Monitoring

"If you want to experience significant progress toward your goal, you need to be intentional about the work you're doing every day."

Anonymous

I remember the days when educators worked tirelessly to "get through" grade level objectives, then give that dreaded end-of-year summative evaluation only to realize that the students did not really learn those objectives. How could that be? We worked so hard! We now realize that it takes more than "getting through" the curriculum to be effective. We also know that **students should be the ones working the hardest in a way that is relevant to them.** We must have a timely and effective way to determine if they are, in fact, grasping the subject matter being taught. It is incumbent upon the educational leader and the professional educators in the classroom to **"inspect what is expected"** on a regular basis, and as a collaborative team, have frank and open discussions on the results. Those discussions should focus on how every student is progressing or not progressing academically; **sharing of successful and unsuccessful practices; and planning for interventions where necessary.**

DuFour and Eaker defined collaboration as *"a systematic process in which we work together, interdependently, to analyze and impact professional practice in order to improve our individual and collective results."*

It is as important to develop common grade level assessments that reflect what students are expected to know. Teachers must be given the opportunity to collaborate and develop a curriculum map reflecting the standards to be taught and a time frame for teaching them. In our climate of high-stakes testing, it is important to ensure those common assessments reflect the standardized assessments that will determine student achievement levels for your school. However, regardless of the high-stakes testing, we must make learning relevant and engaging for our students. Albert Einstein put it best, *"Everything that can be counted doesn't count and everything that counts can't be counted."*

When we determine that certain students are not progressing academically, it is imperative to ensure there are procedures in place to address their needs. As professional educators, we see every child is precious, and their education is critical to the rest of their lives.

Sometimes it is not just the child that may need assistance. As the educational leader it is important to look at the child's instructor to determine if support can be provided. Just as important as student success, we must do everything to ensure the success of our teachers. If teachers are not delivering instruction in the most effective ways, it will be difficult for many of our students to be successful.

Takeaway Assessment and Progress-Monitoring
- **Students should be the ones working the hardest in ways relevant to them.**
- **Educational Leaders must "inspect what they expect."**
- **Professional educators must have the opportunity to share successful practices and plan for student interventions when necessary.**

In the next section we will give an overview of how all the aspects of our efforts came together to make a successful learning environment.

Parents and Students Playing
a Significant Role in the School

"It is easier to build strong children than to repair broken men."

Frederick Douglass

I nvolving families is an integral part of the success of our students. **Parents must be encouraged to be actively involved in their child's education** and ways must be found to encourage them to participate in school activities with their child/children. Families were encouraged to attend our monthly Breakfast with Books, Family Literacy Nights, and Science Fairs. Our school promoted a Multicultural Fair each spring to celebrate the diversity of our school community.

Parent Meetings were held monthly with the administrator to discuss issues relating to our school and the district. A weekly adult computer class offered parents access to ParentLink, homework strategies, and educational websites.

A Schoolwide Behavior Plan and Character Education Program were established. As part of the Schoolwide Behavior Plan, students were asked to recite the Code of Conduct weekly. **A Code of Conduct was created and adopted by all students to promote a safe learning environment.**

The Character Education Program had an important role in promoting positive attitudes in all students. Each month a character trait was selected to represent a positive characteristic that will instill social awareness and an understanding of those students with special needs. The word of the month tied in with our Character Education Assembly. Once a month, selected teachers and support staff performed a play related to the word of the month. Students observed how the characters solved problems and interacted with each other in a positive manner. The objective was for students to apply the skills presented in the play to real-life situations. Students who displayed the positive characteristic throughout the month were chosen by their teacher to be "Tiger of the Month."

The school counselor taught social skills in classrooms, as well as direct teaching in small groups to increase student-to-student relationships and solve problems. Our school also has twenty-six mentors from our community partnership that provided an adult-to-student relationship to build self-esteem and provide a positive adult role model.

Our goal was not only to inspire our students academically, but also to inspire our students to accept the social challenges they may face in the future.

Takeaway from Parents and Students Playing a Significant Role
- **Parents must be encouraged to be actively engaged in the education of their child/children.**
- **Frequent communication with parents is essential.**
- **Parents must be made to understand that the school is also THEIR school.**
- **A school code of conduct and schoolwide behavior plan MUST be established. They should be established with input from the students, parents, and teachers.**

In the next chapter we will discuss how we put it all together as a team of professional educators.

Putting it All Together

"Coming together is a beginning
Staying together is progress
And working together is success."
Henry Ford

At the beginning of the school year, placement tests were given to determine a child's strengths and weakness in the areas of English Language Arts (ELA) and Math. The Tier 3 model was utilized to differentiate instruction for all students. All students received Tier 1 in the classroom. Students in Tier 2 and Tier 3 were given direct instruction by the English Language Learner (ELL) and/or Literacy Specialists in a small group setting. Computer-based programs that were available for all students were Imagine Learning, Study Island, Lexia, and Waterford. All teachers were trained at the beginning of the school year in the Response to Intervention (RTI) model to formulate appropriate interventions for students' needs. Six general education teachers, one resource teacher, the ELL and Literacy Specialists, School Counselor and the School Psychologist were trained to be case managers. The case managers helped the teachers to identify students who were at-risk in the areas of ELA and Math. The case managers and teachers created a target goal and intervention that were observable and measurable to enable the teacher to record the student's progress. Teachers were able to identify students who had not made progress or slow progress in academics through weekly progress-monitoring.

The case manager and teacher met once a week to discuss the student's progress and offer suggestions to increase student learning.

Highly Qualified Sheltered Instruction (HQSI) proved effective for all learners. All teachers were HQSI trained and HQSI strategies were implemented in every classroom. Research showed that when HQSI strategies are in place in the classroom students achieved at a higher academic success rate.

Reciprocal Teaching was another strategy that was effective for all learners to achieve higher comprehension skill in reading and problem-solving. Students benefited from the higher-level questioning, which promotes student academic success. Every day students had an opportunity to work in collaborative groups to discuss, share, and value the interaction of peers who come from different cultures and beliefs.

In-services and New Teacher Training were available on a monthly basis to provide teachers new ways to share and work collaboratively. This collaboration is also an opportunity for all teachers to share best practices and what strategies have proven effective for diverse learners.

Each grade level, K – 5, met at least twice weekly during their Professional Learning Communities (PLCs) to evaluate student work and devise lessons to meet the needs of all learners. Milbrey McLaughlin stated "throughout our ten-year study, whenever we found an effective department within a school, without exception that school or department has been a part of a collaborative Professional Learning Community."

Teachers created monthly ELA and Math formative assessments aligned with the State Standards and Benchmarks to determine which students needed additional help. Once the students were identified, teachers provided the appropriate differentiated Math and ELA skills necessary for student learning according to the assessments.

The resource teacher and general education teacher collaborated to determine what skills and strategies will be in place for the week according to the students' Individualized Education Plan (IEP) and the standards being taught in the classroom. The resource teacher and support staff provided the general education teacher with support in the classroom. The Administrator and Special Education Department met monthly to discuss the interventions in place for our special population and to plan for the continued success of our high-needs students. Even our specialists challenged themselves to provide a positive learning environment. Our school's specialists attended special-education courses in autism and behavior management to improve their classroom instruction to service the needs of all students, including students in our self-contained special-education program. These students spent time in the general education classroom with their age/grade level peers where lessons were taught with respect and compassion.

Epilogue/Conclusion

Building a dedicated, professional team with a common vision was the foundation for success. It was important to face our biases and to use research and facts to determine our direction. Once that direction was decided, staff training and progress-monitoring was essential with everyone in the school understanding and fulfilling their responsibilities. This included the support of parents and building the confidence of our students.

The process outlined and steps taken in this book did not happen overnight. It was not until the fifth year that we saw everything come together for significant improvement in student achievement. Granted we were not the highest achieving school in the district, but we were finally achieving the standards and growth expected by the criteria set by the No Child Left Behind and our state. Our professional team guided our school consisting of a vast majority of children of color, to the status of High Achieving, Exemplary Turn Around, Blue Ribbon Nomination, Numerous Title 1 School of the Year Awards, and above all pride in themselves and their community.

Acknowledgments

Thanks again to my dear wife Regina for her support, encouragement, and love. Thank you to the dedicated professional educators I had the privilege of working with at Twin Lakes Elementary School in sunny Las Vegas, Nevada. You were in fact a family and a consummate group of "Professional Educators." I will always remember you and your dedication to creating a "No Excuse School," and the pride you instilled in our students and the community we served.

Thanks to all the beautiful children that I had the privilege to help guide in this lifetime. You were in fact the highlight of not only my professional career, but also my life. Thanks for allowing me to interact with you on the playground while you were free to run, jump, and have fun. Thank you for playing follow the principal around the playground, asking me to shoot hoops, watching you do tricks on the play set, helping you memorize you First Communion Prayers, and of course, tying your shoes.

It is interesting how God provides lessons for us if only we open our eyes and heart to what is going on around us. One of the greatest miracles I witnessed was seeing children skipping. I thought to myself...wow, I had not skipped in decades. So, I tried it! Well, my legs would not move right, I felt awkward, and bottom line, I looked and felt silly. I wondered what was wrong with me. Why couldn't I skip anymore? As I focused on the children, I noticed something... every child skipping had a smile on their face. Can you imagine how carefree, innocent, and happy you must be to skip? You cannot skip if you are uptight... your body and mind just will not let you.

As I began to wonder what had happened to my skip, I realized that "life had happened to my skip." First, I needed a smile on my face and in my heart. That smile of joy… that feeling in your heart and soul that projects like a warm ray of sunshine that not only brightens your life but also the life of those around you. I noticed that attitude was also an important ingredient to skipping. How positive and carefree the children were as they skipped. They made me realize that I cannot or should not let the everyday pressures consume my life.

"Thank you, children, for reminding me how to skip."

About the Author

D r. Adams is a retired educator, serving parents and students for more than 27 years. Starting in 1987, he performed duties as a classroom teacher, assistant principal, and Highly Qualified Principal. He presented on various educational topics and best practices at the national level including The Council of Great City Schools, Association of Black School Educators, and the National Association of Elementary School Teachers. Presently, Dr. Adams serves in numerous ministries within his church. His community service activities include President of the James B. Knighten Chapter of the Tuskegee Airmen. He is a life member of Omega Psi Phi Fraternity, Inc., and the National Association for the Advancement of Colored People (NAACP). Finally, prior to embarking on a career in education, Dr. Adams served in the United States Air Force from 1976 through 1987, attaining the rank of Captain. He is the recipient of numerous civilian and military awards and honors. Dr. Adams has been married for 39 years to Regina Jones Adams. They have four sons.